# Why isn't Harriette HAIRY YET?

Story and Illustrations by Dr. Kelleyerin Clabaugh

AuthorHouse™
1663 Liberty Drive
Bloomington, IN 47403
www.authorhouse.com
Phone: 833–262–8899

Because of the dynamic nature of the Internet, any web
addresses or links contained in this book may have changed
since publication and may no longer be valid. The views
expressed in this work are solely those of the author and do
not necessarily reflect the views of the publisher, and the
publisher hereby disclaims any responsibility for them.

This book is printed on acid–free paper.

ISBN: 978–1–6655–6611–7 (sc)
ISBN: 978–1–6655–6612–4 (hc)
ISBN: 978–1–6655–6610–0 (e)

Library of Congress Control Number: 2022913599

Print information available on the last page.

Published by AuthorHouse  08/09/2022

authorHOUSE®

# For Torin

May you grow into the beautiful
man you are meant to be.

Your loving Auntie KE

In Zambia there is a place that should
not have to exist but it does...

A place for orphaned baby animals.

Here the humans take care of baby animals
who have lost their families to poachers.

This is where our story begins.

One day a big truck arrived carrying a large crate.

All the animals rushed to see who
their new friend was going to be.

Inside the crate, scared white
eyes stared back at them.

The animals were kind and encouraged
their new friend to come out and play.

Eventually she did and out emerged Harriette.
Harriette was big and bulbous and purpley-pink
and wrinkly and as bald as a baby's bottom.

"What are you?" they asked.

"And where is your hair?"

7

But Harriette did not know the answers.

Her family was gone before she could understand.

The harsh African sun hurt her skin.

She wanted to go back into her crate.

An elegant bird hopped up to her and said

"It's okay. I was bald once too.

I did not have these beautiful
feathers when I was born.

You will grow some soon."

Harriette smiled.

She would love to have beautiful feathers.

So she came out to join her new friends.

But days went by and Harriette
did not grow any feathers.

She had to stay in the water or
cover herself with mud
so her skin would not burn.

Her friend the field mouse said, "Don't worry.

When I was a baby I had pink skin just like you.

And now I am all fuzzy. Just wait!"

So Harriette waited.

But as the days turned into months,
she did not get fuzzier.

And her friends asked each other

"Why isn't Harriette hairy yet?"

Her friend the lion told her

"When I was a baby
I did not have this
thick mane.

You will grow one
too someday."

14

But as more days went by,

Harriette did not grow a thick mane.

And the lion sighed

"Why isn't Harriette hairy yet?"

When she asked to play at night when it was cool
her friends sighed "We are too tired"
and wondered why Harriette wasn't hairy yet.

When she asked them
to play in the water
they exclaimed "We cannot swim!"
And they thought to themselves
"Why isn't Harriette hairy yet?"

One day her friend the kudu shouted
"I see one! I see a hair!"

And sure enough Harriette had grown
a short thick hair on the end of her tail.

"Yeah! Hooray!"

All the animals were excited that Harriette was going to be hairy like them.

But more weeks went by
and Harriette only grew three more
hairs and only on her tail.

The animals frowned.

"Why isn't Harriette hairy yet?"

Harriette was sad.

Why wasn't she like the other animals?

Why didn't she have beautiful feathers?

Was something wrong with her?

One day another truck arrived
with a very large crate.

Out stepped a big grey beast with a long nose.

He was proud and confident and he
was bald just like Harriette!

22

Harriette rushed up
to him and asked

"What are we?

And why aren't we hairy?"

He replied "I am an elephant
and you are a hippo.

We have thick skin so we do
not need hair to protect us.

We are just the way we
are meant to be."

Her new friend was so wise.

Harriette was grateful
she wasn't hairy yet.

All the animals were excited to learn that Harriette was a hippo and she was exactly the way she was meant to be!

So if you feel like Harriette,
Remember you have to have thick skin
when you are different and...

You are just the way you are meant to be!

# Fun Animal Facts:

Hippos actually cannot swim or float.

Instead they hop along
the bottom of the river.

Like their relatives
dolphins and whales,
hippos make clicking noises
underwater to find each other.

Unlike most cats, Lions are social
and live in large family
groups called prides.

The males protect the pride
but the females do the hunting.

Are you brave like a lion?

Greater Kudu are one of the
largest antelope species
and they can jump over 10 feet high!

Only the males have
long spiral horns.

How high can you jump?

Giraffes are the tallest mammals
standing up to 18 feet tall.

Their spots are like fingerprints,
no two giraffe's patterns
are the same.

The African
Crowned Crane is
over 3 feet tall.

This bird likes to
hop and dance.

Can you dance like
a Crowned Crane?

Cheetahs are the
fastest land animals
able to run 70 mph!

How fast can you run?

The Pangolin has a sticky tongue that is as long as its body.

When a Pangolin is scared it rolls up into an armored ball.

What do you do when you are scared?

Elephant are the world's largest land animal.

They grow long teeth called tusks that can weigh up to 240 pounds each!

Do you have really big teeth?

Did you know you helped all
the animals in this book

by reading about them?

Harriette and her friends are lucky
to have a friend like you!

Thank you, Mahalo, Zikomo

Printed in the United States
by Baker & Taylor Publisher Services